SIMONE BILES

Jon M. Fishman

Lerner Publications ◆ Minneapolis

Copyright © 2017 by Lerner Publishing Group, Inc.

All rights reserved. International copyright secured. No part of this book may be reproduced, stored in a retrieval system, or transmitted in any form or by any means—electronic, mechanical, photocopying, recording, or otherwise—without the prior written permission of Lerner Publishing Group, Inc., except for the inclusion of brief quotations in an acknowledged review.

Lerner Publications Company
A division of Lerner Publishing Group, Inc.
241 First Avenue North
Minneapolis, MN 55401 USA

For reading levels and more information, look up this title at www.lernerbooks.com.

Main body text set in Albany Std 15/22. Typeface provided by Agfa.

Library of Congress Cataloging-in-Publication Data

Names: Fishman, Jon M., author.
Title: Simone Biles / Jon M. Fishman.
Description: Minneapolis : Lerner Publications, [2017] | Series: Sports All-Stars
    | Includes bibliographical references and index. | Audience: Ages: 7–11. |
    Audience: Grades: 4 to 6.
Identifiers: LCCN 2016039209 (print) | LCCN 2016041149 (ebook) |
    ISBN 9781512448979 (lb : alk. paper) | ISBN 9781512448986 (pb : alk. paper) |
    ISBN 9781512448993 (eb pdf)
Subjects: LCSH: Biles, Simone, 1997——Juvenile literature. | Gymnasts—United
    States—Biography—Juvenile literature. | Women gymnasts—United States—
    Biography—Juvenile literature.
Classification: LCC GV460.2.B55 F57 2017 (print) | LCC GV460.2.B55 (ebook) |
    DDC 796.44092 [B] —dc23

LC record available at https://lccn.loc.gov/2016039209

Manufactured in the United States of America
1-42826-26500-9/28/2016

CONTENTS

Gold Getter. 4

Learning to Soar 8

Training a Champion 12

Off the Mat 18

"The First Simone Biles" 22

All-Star Stats 28

Source Notes 29

Glossary 30

Further Information 31

Index 32

GOLD GETTER

Simone Biles on the balance beam during the 2016 Olympic Games

US gymnast Simone Biles crouched on the **balance beam.** With her arms raised, she spun on one foot two and a half times. Biles danced on the 4-inch-wide (10-centimeter) beam. She flipped gracefully across it. Through it all, she kept her balance, never once losing her footing or slipping from the beam.

Biles and her teammates were competing in the 2016 Olympic Games in Rio de Janeiro, Brazil. They were leading the women's **team final**. Balance beam was the third of four events in the final. If Biles could get a top score, the team would be in a great position to win a gold medal.

All that was left for Biles on the balance beam was the **dismount**. She flipped backward twice. She launched herself from the end of the beam and spun and twisted in the air. Her teammates cheered when Biles landed on her feet. She had the best balance beam score of the day!

Many gymnastics fans expected the United States to win the women's final. The biggest reason was Simone Biles. She had won three world **all-around** titles in a row from 2013 to 2015. Lots of big names in gymnastics were calling her the best gymnast of all time.

Biles flips across the balance beam during the women's team final at the 2016 Olympic Games.

Gymnasts practice their moves over and over. They spend hundreds of hours in the gym to get ready for a big **meet**. But many still crack under the pressure when judges are watching. Not Biles. One of her great strengths is staying cool and calm in the spotlight.

The **floor exercise** was the last event of the day. All eyes in the arena were on Biles. Millions of fans watched on TV as she

Biles competes in the team floor exercise.

flew across the mat. No one in women's gymnastics can soar as high as she can. She celebrated with her coach and teammates when it was finished. The United States had won the gold medal!

The team's final victory wasn't the end of the Olympics for Biles. She would compete in the all-around and three other events. In all, she had a chance to win five medals. Biles was out to prove again that she was the top gymnast in the world.

Biles performs a floor routine in 2013.

Simone Biles was born on March 14, 1997, in Columbus, Ohio. She grew up in Spring, Texas, with her younger sister, Adria, after the girls were adopted by their grandparents. Both sisters loved to jump and tumble. Simone taught herself to flip backward off a mailbox. One day, her day care group went on a field trip to a gym. Simone saw gymnasts practicing their **routines**. The young girl copied them by trying her own moves.

Simone's adoptive parents, Ron and Nellie, received a letter a short time later. It was from the gym. One of the coaches had noticed Simone flipping and rolling. The coach suggested Simone start practicing at the gym. Ron and Nellie agreed that gymnastics would be a great fit for their daughter.

Biles with her mom and dad, Nellie and Ron, in 2016.

About one year later, Simone began working with Aimee Boorman. The coach believed in Simone's talent and thought she could be great in the gym. But Boorman had never worked with a top-level gymnast before. "We were both kind of clueless about it," Simone said. "So we were just learning together."

Simone learned fast. By the age of 10, she was competing against top gymnasts her age from around the country. She was at the junior **elite** level four years later. Two years after that, Simone burst onto the international gymnastics scene in a big way. She had the top scores at the 2013 world championships to take the all-around title. Her floor exercise really wowed the crowd. "On floor, I just have a lot of fun," Simone said. "That is the main key."

Biles competes on floor exercise in 2012.

Aimee Boorman gives advice to Biles before a competition in 2016. Boorman began coaching Biles in 2003.

Being named 2013 world champion was just the beginning for Simone. She won the title again in 2014. Then, in 2015, she won the all-around world championship for the third year in a row. She became the first woman to win the world title three straight times. In 2016, she would get her chance to add Olympic medals to her trophy case.

Training at the gym helps Biles to build muscle.

Biles performs her signature move on floor exercise—a backwards double flip with a half twist landing.

Simone Biles has ruled the highest level of gymnastics since 2013. She's a world champion and an Olympic champion. She even has a floor exercise move named after her. She's brimming with athletic talent. But to stay on top, talent isn't enough. She works *really* hard.

In 2013, Biles's lower leg was sore after she landed a certain way. She and Coach Boorman came up with a new way to land. The new way felt better, but it wasn't easy. The new move became known as the Biles, and it's in the official gymnastics rule book.

Biles spends 32 hours each week training in the gym. She spreads that time over six days. Stretching her muscles is a big part of her daily workout. Stretching helps prevent injury. It also allows Biles's arms and legs to reach the extreme positions her routines call for. She stretches on her own and with coaches and teammates.

Part of Biles's time in the gym is spent practicing basic skills. These include the flips and spins that make up her routines. To make a skill perfect, Biles does it over and over and over again. When it comes time to perform in a meet, she barely has to think about the skill to do it just right.

Biles stays focused during training.

Biles (center) trains with her teammates.

Cardio training is another part of Biles's workouts. Coach Boorman doesn't want her star athlete to get tired during a meet. In the gym, Biles will practice a skill such as backflips. Then she'll run back to where she started and do it again without pausing. Cardio training makes her heart and lungs strong.

To get ready for a meet, Biles puts her skills together to create a routine. She links her flips and twists with leaps and turns. She practices to make sure everything works together. At the meet, Biles will be judged in part by how smoothly her routine flows.

Coach Boorman trusts Biles to eat healthful food. The gymnast knows that if she doesn't eat well, she won't perform well. That means lots of egg whites, fish, and chicken. Before a workout, she eats bananas with peanut butter. Biles says the snack helps prevent muscle cramps.

Biles works on her balance beam skills by doing flips.

Sometimes Biles throws out her food plan. She likes soda and other snacks. And after a big meet, it's time to celebrate! "It doesn't even matter if I don't win. . . . After every meet I have pizza. Pepperoni pizza."

Biles attends the 2016 MTV Video Music Awards.

Biles's friends and family don't think of her as a superstar athlete.

At home, she does chores, laughs with her parents, and argues with her sister. She also plays with the family's four German shepherd

Biles began to go to school at home at the age of 13. Learning at home helped her keep up with her gym schedule. But she didn't like it. She missed seeing her friends every day.

dogs: Maggie, Atlas, Bella, and Lily. She loves to shop and get her nails done. And she still has sleepovers with her friends.

Biles says her favorite food is Italian, and she loves to eat at Olive Garden. She likes the TV show *Pretty Little Liars* and the *Hunger Games* books. She dances to new songs on the radio. When she's with her friends, Biles is a lot like most young women.

To the rest of the world, Biles is a star on and off the mat. She appeared on the cover of *Sports Illustrated* and other magazines. She has been on TV shows such as *Fox and Friends*, the *Ellen DeGeneres Show*, and *Today*.

The members of the US women's gymnastics team appear on the *Today* show during the 2016 Olympics. *From left*: Biles, Laurie Hernandez, Aly Raisman, Madison Kocian, and Gabby Douglas.

During the 2016 Olympics, Biles said she had a crush on Zac Efron. She admitted to having a cardboard cutout of the actor in her room at home. The *Today* show came up with an idea. They flew Efron to Brazil to surprise Biles! She was thrilled to meet him. The two talked and took photos together. They even exchanged friendly kisses!

(1.9 m) tall.

Her height has never slowed her down. In fact, Biles is only about 1 inch (2.5 cm) shorter than the average elite female gymnast. Being short can help athletes perform better spins and flips. In 2016, it helped Biles become an Olympic champion. The smallest member of Team USA carried the flag for her country at the closing ceremony in Rio de Janeiro.

Biles carries the US flag during the Olympics closing ceremony.

"THE FIRST SIMONE BILES"

Biles gives a gold medal performance with her floor routine.

The 2016 Olympics was a huge success for the United States and Biles. They had already won gold in the team event. But many fans consider the all-around event to be the biggest prize in a gymnastics meet. Biles was a huge favorite to win it in Brazil.

Biles keeps her eye on the bar during the all-around event.

But after two events in the all-around, Biles was in second place. This wasn't how it was supposed to go. Russia's Aliya Mustafina had taken first place with a great **uneven bars** routine. Then Biles came roaring back on the balance beam. She nailed her routine, while Mustafina lost her balance. The floor exercise was last. Biles leaped and soared with joy. When she finished, she was named Olympic all-around champion!

Biles twists in the air during her individual vault event.

Biles waves to the crowd during a medal ceremony. She won one bronze and four gold medals at the Rio Olympics.

Biles went on to win gold medals in the floor exercise and **vault** events. She won a bronze medal on the balance beam for a total of five Olympic medals. That made it one of the most successful Olympics ever for a US athlete. Fans compared her to some of the greatest Olympians of all time. "I'm not a celebrity," she said. "I'm not the next Usain Bolt or Michael Phelps. I'm the first Simone Biles."

Biles holds a box of Kellogg's cereal featuring Team USA. The group will go on a national tour sponsored by Kellogg's.

Biles and her teammates planned to join the Kellogg's Tour of Gymnastics Champions after the Olympics. The tour would visit 36 cities in the United States, bringing world-class gymnastics to the fans. After spending months together training for the Olympics, Biles and her teammates would get to be together for a bit longer.

Fans wanted to know if Biles would return for the next Summer Olympics. The games are planned for Tokyo, Japan, in 2020. In an interview, Biles said she planned to take a vacation after the Olympics and the Kellogg's Tour. Then she was going to head back to the gym to train—and a trip to Tokyo for Biles seems very likely.

Biles is welcomed home with a parade in Spring, Texas.

All-Star Stats

Gymnasts from the United States have been winning a lot at the Olympics. Take a look at the women's team final and all-around winners from recent Olympics.

All-Around Gold-Medal Winners

2016 Simone Biles, United States
2012 Gabby Douglas, United States
2008 Nastia Liukin, United States
2004 Carly Patterson, United States
2000 Simona Amanar, Romania
1996 Lilia Podkopayeva, Ukraine

Team Final Gold-Medal-Winning Country

2016 United States
2012 United States
2008 China
2004 Romania
2000 Romania
1996 United States

Source Notes

10 Julia Fincher, "Who Is . . . Simone Biles," *NBCOlympics.com*, July 29, 2016, http://www .nbcolympics.com/news/who-simone-biles.

10 Associated Press, "Simone Biles Crowned Gymnastics All-Around World Champion," Team USA, October 4, 2013, http://www.teamusa.org /News/2013/October/04/Simone-Biles-Crowned -Gymnastics-All-Around-World-Champion.

17 Caroline Praderio, "Here's What Simone Biles Eats before and after She Competes," *Business Insider*, August 12, 2016, http://mobile.businessinsider.com /simone-biles-diet-2016-8.

25 James Masters, "Simone Biles Wins All-Around Gold at Rio Games in US One-Two," *CNN*, last modified August 12, 2016, http://edition.cnn.com/2016/08/11 /sport/simone-biles-usa-gymnastics-rio/.

Glossary

all-around: a competition in which female gymnasts compete alone on vault, uneven bars, balance beam, and floor exercise

balance beam: a narrow beam on which gymnasts perform. This is also the name of an event in gymnastics.

cardio: a type of workout designed to get the heart pumping and improve blood flow

dismount: to get down from something, such as a balance beam

elite: the top level of gymnastics

floor exercise: an event in which gymnasts perform on an open floor

meet: a large competition with many gymnastics events

routines: combinations of skills

team final: a competition in which female gymnasts compete as a team on vault, uneven bars, balance beam, and floor exercise

uneven bars: an event in which gymnasts perform on two bars, one high and one low

vault: an event in which gymnasts launch from a springboard to a vaulting table and then into the air

Further Information

Fishman, Jon M. *Michael Phelps*. Minneapolis: Lerner Publications, 2017.

Herman, Gail. *What Are the Summer Olympics?* New York: Grosset & Dunlap, 2016.

Instagram: Simone Biles
https://www.instagram.com/simonebiles/?hl=en

Rio 2016
https://www.rio2016.com/en

Savage, Jeff. *Usain Bolt*. Minneapolis: Lerner Publications, 2013.

USA Gymnastics
https://usagym.org

Index

all-around, 6–7, 11, 22–23

balance beam, 5–6, 17, 23, 25

Biles, Adria, 8

Biles, Nellie, 9

Biles, Ron, 9

Biles, the, 14

Boorman, Aimee, 10, 11, 14, 16–17

Efron, Zac, 20

floor exercise, 7, 10, 13, 23, 25

Kellogg's Tour of Gymnastics Champions, 26–27

Mustafina, Aliya, 23

Phelps, Michael, 21, 25

Rio de Janeiro, 5, 21, 25

team final, 5, 6

uneven bars, 23

vault, 25

Photo Acknowledgments

The images in this book are used with the permission of: © iStockphoto.com/iconeer (gold stars); TERRY SCHMITT/UPI/Newscom, p. 2; © Bob Martin/Sports Illustrated/ Getty Images, pp. 4, 5, 6, 7; © Tim Clayton/Corbis/Getty Images, p. 8; © Kohjiro Kinno/Sports Illustrated/Getty Images, p. 9; Richard Ulereich/ZUMAPRESS/ Newscom, p. 10; © Maddie Meyer/Getty Images, p. 11; AP Photo/Rex Features, pp. 12, 23, 25; © Kyodo News/Getty Images, pp. 13, 22; David Drufke/ZUMA Press/ Newscom, p. 15; AP Photo/David J. Phillip, pp. 16, 17; © Nicholas Hunt/Getty Images, p. 18; © Harry How/Getty Images, p. 20; AP Photo/Matt Dunham, p. 21; Mike Blake/ Reuters/Newscom, p. 24; AP Photo/Amy Sussman for Kellogg's, p. 26; AP Photo/ Michael Ciaglo/Houston Chronicle, p. 27.

Front cover: TERRY SCHMITT/UPI/Newscom; iStockphoto.com/neyro2008 (motion lines); © iStockphoto.com/ulimi (black and white stars).